W9-CLV-071

3 1526 04468830 4

Growing Good Food

Anne Flounders

RED CHAIR
·PRESS·

Please visit our website at **www.redchairpress.com**.
Find a free catalog of all our high-quality products for young readers.

Growing Good Food

Publisher's Cataloging-In-Publication Data
(Prepared by The Donohue Group, Inc.)

Flounders, Anne.

Growing good food / Anne Flounders.
p. : ill., maps ; cm. -- (Our green Earth)
Summary: In this book, you'll find out why community-supported agriculture is growing fast and how the choices you make at the grocery store can make a big difference in Earth's health as well as your own. Includes step-by-step ideas for taking action, different points of view, an up-close look at relevant careers, and more.
Includes bibliographical references and index.
ISBN: 978-1-939656-43-8 (lib. binding/hardcover)
ISBN: 978-1-939656-31-5 (pbk.)
ISBN: 978-1-939656-50-6 (eBook)
1. Community-supported agriculture--Environmental aspects--Juvenile literature. 2. Organic farming--Environmental aspects--Juvenile literature. 3. Natural foods--Juvenile literature. 4. Agriculture--Environmental aspects. 5. Organic farming. 6. Natural foods. I. Title.
HD1491.A3 F56 2014

334/.683   2013937162

Copyright © 2014 Red Chair Press LLC

All rights reserved. No part of this book may be reproduced, stored in an information or retrieval system, or transmitted in any form by any means, electronic, mechanical including photocopying, recording, or otherwise without the prior written permission from the Publisher. For permissions, contact info@redchairpress.com

Illustration credit: p.12: Joe LeMonnier

Photo credits: Cover, title page, TOC, p. 4, 5, 7, 8, 9, 10, 13, 14, 15, 16, 18, 19, 20, 22, 23, 24, 25, 26, 27, 31, back cover: Shutterstock; p. 5, 21: Keith Garton; p. 6, 7, 11, 22, 23: Dreamstime; p. 17: James B. Casey; p. 28, 29: Terri Langley; p.32: © Hildi Todrin, Crane Song Photography

This series first published by:
Red Chair Press LLC   PO Box 333   South Egremont, MA 01258-0333

Printed in the United States of America

1 2 3 4 5 18 17 16 15 14

MIX
Paper from
responsible sources
FSC
www.fsc.org   FSC® C002589

TABLE OF CONTENTS

CHAPTER ONE

Food From the Earth

Walk through the produce aisles of a grocery store. Our eyes are treated to a rainbow of color. Fruits and vegetables of all shapes, sizes, and colors await us. The apples may have come from Washington. The cherries may have come from Michigan. The grapes may have come from California. The oranges may have come from Florida. They all have one thing in common. They all came from the Earth.

Fruits and vegetables, like all plants, need air, water, and soil to grow. Clean air, clean water, and clean soil help plants stay healthy. That seems like a simple enough idea. But the food system in America is not quite so simple.

Over the past few decades, the population in the United States has grown. So has the demand for a large variety of fruits and vegetables to be available all year round. How do farmers meet that demand? How do they grow so much food? How does it get to the grocery store?

Fruits and vegetables are healthy for us. But some ways of growing food and getting it to people are better for Earth than are other ways. Knowing a bit about the food system can help people make decisions when they buy these foods.

Farmers today produce 260 percent more food than in 1950.

DID YOU KNOW?
The number-one crop in the United States is corn. The U.S. grows more corn than any other country in the world. But only about 12 percent of this corn is eaten by people. Most of it goes to feed animals.

That's Bananas!

Quick quiz: What's the most popular fruit in the United States?

The answer is the banana. The average American eats between 25 and 30 pounds of bananas a year. The banana has many things going for it. It is packed with vitamins and other important nutrients. A single banana can be bought for about a quarter in many places.

Most bananas that we eat today are grown in Central and South America. Banana **plantations** thrive in warm climates near the Equator. Bananas can be grown year round. This is important because world demand for the fruit is very high.

It takes about nine months to grow bananas. The plants are kept constantly watered. Banana plants need 36 liters of water per day. The water used to keep the bananas needs to go somewhere, too. Extra water is pumped out of the plantation. This is a typical system for any kind of farm. A watering system on a farm is called **irrigation**. The system for waste water is called **drainage**.

Banana plantations use water in storage basins.

The people who grow bananas don't want bugs or plant diseases to ruin the fruit. There are many steps they can take to protect the bananas. The plants are watered often as the bananas grow. After the bananas are picked, they are packed carefully for shipping. They are put into refrigerated containers. Then they are sent to their final destination. Along the way they could travel by ship, truck, and train to almost anywhere in the world.

Bananas are washed and sorted before being packed.

The story of how a banana grows and ends up in a lunchbox is part of a larger story. That story is the **food system**. Every food is part of the food system. Bananas are just one food among thousands that are planted, grown, picked, and shipped. A closer look at the food system shows its very close relationship to the health of the Earth.

DID YOU KNOW?

Three-quarters of the water used in the world is for farming. About two-thirds of that water is lost through evaporation and faulty irrigation.

CHAPTER TWO

The Food System

A lunchbox might hold a sandwich with bread baked in Connecticut, chicken salad made in Kentucky, and mustard from France. The ingredients for the bread, chicken salad, and mustard likely came from somewhere else entirely. Usually, each food's story is a bit of a mystery to the consumer. Where did the food come from? Where was it processed? How did it get to my plate? The answers lie in the food system.

Large tractors and machines help farmers harvest our food.

Our Food System

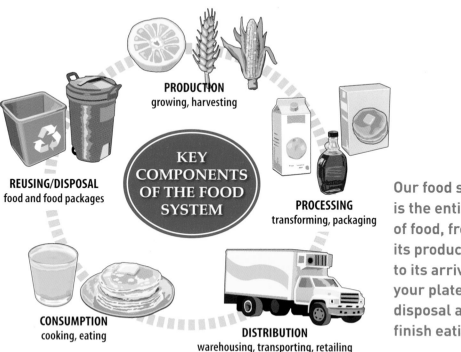

PRODUCTION
growing, harvesting

KEY COMPONENTS OF THE FOOD SYSTEM

REUSING/DISPOSAL
food and food packages

PROCESSING
transforming, packaging

CONSUMPTION
cooking, eating

DISTRIBUTION
warehousing, transporting, retailing

Our food system is the entire story of food, from its production to its arrival on your plate, to its disposal after you finish eating.

Source: Greater Kansas City Food Coalition

There are so many food choices. How can a person make a choice about food that is not only healthy for the person, but also healthy for Earth? We might not know each individual food's whole story. But knowing more about the food system can help people make good green choices.

Agriculture is the science and practice of producing food from the Earth. That may mean growing plants for food. It may mean raising animals for meat, dairy, or eggs. All of these are closely tied to the Earth. All plants and animals need land, air, and water to grow.

Farms are big. They need to produce a lot of food. About 914 million acres of land in the U.S. are used for agriculture. That's more land than the entire western U.S.[1] Producing and harvesting large amounts of food on so much land requires fossil

Trucks collect grain from wheat and crop harvesters.

fuels. Fuels are used to run farm machinery. Chemicals made from fossil fuels are used to feed crops. They also prevent weeds and bugs from killing crops. The chemicals can get into the soil and water surrounding the farm.

Using fossil fuels puts greenhouse gases into the air. Greenhouse gases get trapped in the atmosphere and lead to global warming and climate change. One problem related to climate change is **drought**. Drought is when there is little or no rain in an area. Rivers and ponds dry out. Water is needed for crops to grow. A major drought in 2012 killed many crops throughout the United States.

Drought makes it difficult for crops to grow like in this Illinois cornfield.

[1] Source: U.S. Department of Agriculture

Green Growth

There are two main ways food can be grown. One way is using conventional agriculture. That means using the standard practices of a large-scale farm. Conventional farming is used to grow a large amount of food quickly. It can meet a high demand. Chemicals are commonly used on crops to help them grow.

Many people worry that these chemicals are not healthy for Earth. They also worry people will get sick if the chemicals are still on the food when it is eaten. Some chemicals have been linked to cancer and other diseases. The government tests samples of food to make sure it is safe.

A low-flying plane sprays chemicals over a farm field.

Some farmers use a mix of chemical fertilizer and manure.

The Dirty Dozen/The Clean Fifteen

   An organization called the Environmental Working Group tested conventional fruits and vegetables. Some had more chemicals left on them than others. Based on their findings, the group suggests which fruits and vegetables to buy organic (the ones that held the most chemicals) and which were okay to buy non-organic (the ones that held the least chemicals).

The Dirty Dozen
Best to buy organic

1. Apples
2. Bell peppers
3. Blueberries
4. Celery
5. Cucumbers
6. Grapes
7. Lettuce
8. Nectarines
9. Peaches
10. Potatoes
11. Spinach
12. Strawberries

The Clean Fifteen
Okay to buy non-organic

1. Asparagus
2. Avocado
3. Cabbage
4. Cantaloupe
5. Corn
6. Eggplant
7. Grapefruit
8. Kiwi
9. Mangoes
10. Mushrooms
11. Onions
12. Pineapples
13. Sweet Peas
14. Sweet Potatoes
15. Watermelon

Source: The Environmental Working Group

Organic Farming

The other way food can be grown is by using **organic** methods. About two percent of the food grown in the United States is organic. Organic farmers do not use the chemicals that conventional farmers

Some home growers use organic methods.

use. Crops are grown using natural methods. People who choose organic foods are making a choice to stay away from the chemicals used in conventional farming.

Organic farming is better for soil and water. Natural **fertilizers** help crops grow and add nutrients to the soil. That makes

soil

Inside a compost bin

the soil richer over time. It also keeps dangerous chemicals out of the water around the farm. That's better for Earth and for the animals and people who use the water.

Many organic farmers use **compost** when planting crops. Compost is organic matter, such as food and leaves. The organic matter naturally breaks down. It becomes a healthful addition to the soil where plants grow.

Why isn't every farm an organic farm? One reason is because organic crops are more likely to be ruined by pests. Natural methods can keep some pests out. But chemicals do a more complete job. Conventional farming produces more food. Also, organic farming can be more expensive for the farmer. That means the food may cost more at the market.

COLLEGE TO CAREER

Do you think you might be interested in a career in organic or sustainable agriculture?

Here are just a few of the jobs you could do.

Cheese Maker	*Ranch Manager*
Land Policy Researcher	*Seed Manager*
Nutrition Coordinator	*Community Educator*

"Think about it. You work on a CSA* farm with 2 acres of land. You have 250 members who expect a box of produce every week. You have to decide how many plants serve everyone and how much space each occupies." This is one example of the math farmers use every day

JESSE NAYLOR

says Jesse Naylor, organic agriculture student at Washington State University. "Community farming lets people get up close to how and where their food is grown." As a career goal, Jesse hopes to bring the benefits of sustainable farming to developing countries in Africa.

*Community-Supported Agriculture

Getting Food from Here to There

How far does food travel before it is eaten? This distance is sometimes referred to as food miles. Often, people don't know exactly how far food has traveled. Sometimes there are clues. Look for stickers on fruits and vegetables. The stickers may tell where the food was grown.

Food often has to travel a long distance. For example, bananas may come from Central and South America. That is the best place to grow them. Studies have shown that the average American meal travels about 1,500 miles before it is eaten.[2]

Food may be shipped by truck, ship, or train. They may be short trips or long trips. Transportation, of course, uses fossil fuels. But even more fossil fuels are used in refrigerating food that travels long distances. Transportation accounts for about 2.5 percent of the food system's greenhouse gas emissions. Refrigeration, on the other hand, accounts for 18 percent.

That's why many people like to buy local food when they can. Local food is grown or produced within about a day's drive from one's home. Because it does not have to travel far, local food is often fresher than food that travels a long distance. But it does still need to travel, so it still uses fossil fuels. Local food options may be very limited, depending on the area.

[2] Source: Clemson University

FACE OFF: The Apple Question

You're at a supermarket in New York looking at huge piles of apples. What is the better choice: The organic apple all the way from New Zealand? Or the conventionally-grown apple from a farm about 100 miles from the store?

"I would choose the organic apple. I like the idea of growing food without chemicals that might make me sick. Organic food seems like it's better for me."

Organic and conventional apples have the same nutritional content. But people worry about the chemicals used to manage pests on farms. Some have been shown to make people sick. Organic farming practices keep the air and water around the farm cleaner than conventional farming. For that reason, the organic apple is healthier for Earth, too.

"I would go for the local apple. It's probably fresher than the apple that came from halfway around the world. And because it didn't have to travel very far, it used fewer fossil fuels to get to the store than the organic apple did."

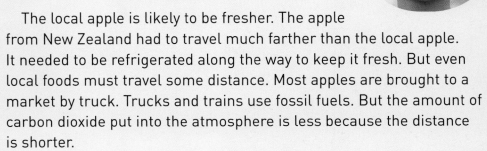

The local apple is likely to be fresher. The apple from New Zealand had to travel much farther than the local apple. It needed to be refrigerated along the way to keep it fresh. But even local foods must travel some distance. Most apples are brought to a market by truck. Trucks and trains use fossil fuels. But the amount of carbon dioxide put into the atmosphere is less because the distance is shorter.

Which would you choose?

CHAPTER · THREE

People and Food

People who try to eat well and protect Earth might like to eat all local and organic foods. But that's just not possible for most of us. So people try to make good decisions about food when they can. What are some food choices that are healthy for people and for Earth?

This chef in Hillsdale, NY, uses foods grown only by local growers.

Markets like this one in Evanston, Illinois, are a good source for locally grown foods.

Farmers' Markets

A great place to get local and seasonal food is a farmers' market. There are farmers' markets all over the world. They are even in big cities. Farmers come to sell fresh fruits, vegetables, eggs, meat, herbs, honey, jam, breads, and more. The people selling the food can tell customers what is fresh that week. Some of the fruits and vegetables may have been picked that day! There is often an amazing variety of food available. Much of the food sold at a farmers' market is organic, too.

At a farmers' market, it can be fun to meet the people who grow the foods you eat.

Most stands at a farmers' market name the farm where the food came from. It is usually not far from the market. This is one chapter of the food system story that is not a mystery!

Community-Supported Agriculture

Community-supported agriculture. Those are three big words and one big idea. People often call it CSA. A CSA is a way for people to buy fresh, local, organic food straight from the farm.

People buy a "share" in a local farm ahead of the growing season. In exchange, the farmer provides them with a fresh box of in-season food each week. The boxes typically have fruits and vegetables in them. Some CSAs also include eggs, flowers, or other products.

Usually, the members of a CSA don't know exactly what they will get from week to week. It's a seasonal surprise. But members always know exactly where their food has come from. Many CSAs even allow their members to pick their own food right from the farm fields.

DID YOU KNOW?

The idea of community-supported agriculture has its roots in Japan. It was introduced in 1965, and it was given the name teikei. That means "food with the farmer's face on it."

Grow Your Own Food

You cannot get much more local than growing your own food at home. Once you start, you may find you want to keep growing more! Here is how you can start your own super-local farm.

Step 1: Get a packet of seeds. Don't want to wait long for your first harvest? Quick-growing plants include radishes, peas, carrots, lettuce, or herbs.

Step 2: Decide where you will plant. It could be a sunny space outside. You could use a sunny windowsill. Be sure to give each plant plenty of room to grow. Try just one plant or two plants to begin with if you aren't sure how much space you will need.

Step 3: Use a rake or shovel to turn over the soil. Get rid of any rocks and weeds. Check your soil. Vegetables grow best in loam. That is a brown soil that is moist and sticks together when you squeeze it. If your soil is very dry or red, you may need to improve it with compost and fertilizer. If you use a container, use fresh potting soil.

Step 4: Plant and water the seeds according to the seed packet directions. Outdoor plants get about an inch of water a week. If it rains, that counts as watering!

Step 5: Pull weeds from your garden regularly.

Step 6: Wait for your garden to grow. Be sure to wash your food well before eating. Enjoy!

Urban Farms

Concrete sidewalks; brick buildings; tomatoes on a vine. Is one of these things out of place? Not at all! In cities across the United States, people are

A green roof garden

reclaiming empty parcels of land to grow their own food. These plots are called urban farms. They're not just on the ground, either. Some urban farms are on rooftops.

Urban farms are good for a community *and* good for Earth. The farms and gardens can make use of compost made from food waste. That reduces the amount of waste that a neighborhood produces. The plants can also improve the air quality in a neighborhood.

Some city neighborhoods are called food deserts. That means there are not enough stores that sell fresh, healthful food. Urban farms are especially important in these neighborhoods. They allow people to grow their own food together right in their own local community.

An empty city lot doesn't look very nice. With urban farms, people work together to prepare the land to grow good, healthful food.

Farm to School

Many schools are serving healthy locally grown food at lunch time. These are called Farm to School programs. More than 10,000 schools in all fifty states are part of a Farm to School program. Oregon schools serve apples, potatoes, radishes, pears, cranberries, corn, and marionberries grown right in the state. They also serve local milk and bread. Massachusetts students are eating local apples, collard greens, squash, strawberries, rutabagas, and sweet potatoes. Georgia students are eating locally-grown apples, lettuce, broccoli, carrots, green beans, strawberries, squash, and watermelon. Each state has its own variety of fruits, vegetables, beans, dairy, and grains.

Eating locally grown foods is good for you and for Earth.

More people want to know the stories behind the food they eat. They also want to become a bigger part of that story. They are doing that by growing their own food or buying local or organic food. That helps cut down on the use of fossil fuels and chemicals that may harm the planet and people. Choosing local and organic food when possible can help keep the Earth and its people healthy.

On The Job

Name: Terri Langley

Job: Farm to Fork Coordinator, MA'O Organic Farms, Waianae, Hawaii

What do you do as a Farm to Fork Coordinator?

Terri Langley: My job is to empower young folks to make healthy, sustainable food choices, and to respect and honor the land. The Hawaiian concepts of *kanu* (plant), *malama* (nurture), and *ai* (to eat) allow me to teach students through activities that stimulate discovery and create lasting memories and experiences. I teach students where their food comes from, and why it's important to use proper food-growing techniques that preserve and respect our resources.

How did you become interested in working with food?

TL: After traveling around the world, I realized that every culture had food in common. And many cultures had an intimate and significant relationship to the manner of growing food and the treatment of their land. I knew I wanted to be in the food industry. After moving to Hawaii, I began to expand my plant knowledge and experiment with cooking. I worked in nurseries and composting facilities. Then I became an organic farm inspector, a master gardener, a master preserver, and owned a small café, specializing in local foods. It was through these activities, that I ended up here at MA'O Organic Farms, working with students.

What types of food do you grow?

TL: MA'O is a 24-acre certified organic fruit and vegetable farm. We grow lots of greens: Asian, spinach, lettuces, and bitters. Also kale, collards, chards, herbs, carrots, Japanese radish- Hakurei, beets, cabbage, fennel, eggplant, taro, banana, citrus, mango, and papaya. My direct responsibility is the chef's garden, where we grow all the farm vegetables. The chef's garden is where the experimenting happens; it's also our outdoor lab and activity zone.

What is a typical day at work for you?

TL: A typical Farm to Fork visit might look like this: Twenty-five eager students arrive by bus for a three-hour visit. We first introduce ourselves to this land and its ancestors. Then begin the farm tour [to learn about] organic and sustainable farming practices. We walk through post-harvest practices: washing, grading, packaging, and delivery. It is now time for our *hana*, the service part of the visit. So we go into our chef's garden and do an activity related to planting. We make sure we harvest some food, because our next step is the kitchen where we learn to prepare what we have harvested. Then we eat! Before they leave,

I give each student a package of seeds to grow at home with their family.

Why are organic farming and local food so important?

TL: I talk a lot about the benefits of local food systems in terms of safety, resources, and community building, but my parting message and seed give-away is simple: **Grow something and eat it.** I tell students that if you do this with the seeds I give you, a secret will be unveiled to you, and will bring you knowledge. The secret, of course, being the secret of life, and the beautiful knowledge of growing good food.

Check it out: maoorganicfarms.org

Glossary

agriculture   the science and practice of producing food

compost   natural matter, such as leaves and food waste, that is broken down into a rich material that can be added to soil

drainage   the act or method of removing excess water from an area

drought   a long period of time in which there is much less rainfall than is normal

fertilizer   a substance added to soil to help plants grow

food system   the process of producing, shipping, processing, packaging, consuming, and disposing of food

irrigation   the process of adding water to crops

organic   food or the production of foods without the use of chemicals, pesticides, or other artificial agents

plantation   an area where many plants are grown together

FOR MORE INFORMATION

Books

Bloomfield, Jill. *Grow It, Cook It.* DK Publishing, 2008.

Goodman, Polly. *Food, Farming and the Future.* Gareth Stevens Publishing, 2012.

Rand, Casey. *Producing Vegetables.* (The Technology of Farming Series). Heinemann, 2013.

Web Sites

Farm to School Network: *Read how schools and local farms work together to provide good food for over 5 million kids in the U.S.*
www.farmtoschool.org

Local Harvest: *Find farms, farmers' markets, and community-supported agriculture programs in your area.*
www.localharvest.org

What's On Your Plate? Project: *Test your good-foods knowledge.*
www.whatsonyourplateproject.org/games

All web addresses (URLs) have been reviewed carefully by our editors. Web sites change, however, and we cannot guarantee that a site's future contents will continue to meet our high standards of quality and educational value.

INDEX

About the Author

Anne Flounders has lots of on-the-job experience writing for kids and teens. She has written and edited magazines, nonfiction books, teachers' guides, reader's theater plays, and web content. She has also recorded narration for audio- and ebooks. Anne protects our green Earth with her husband and son in Connecticut.